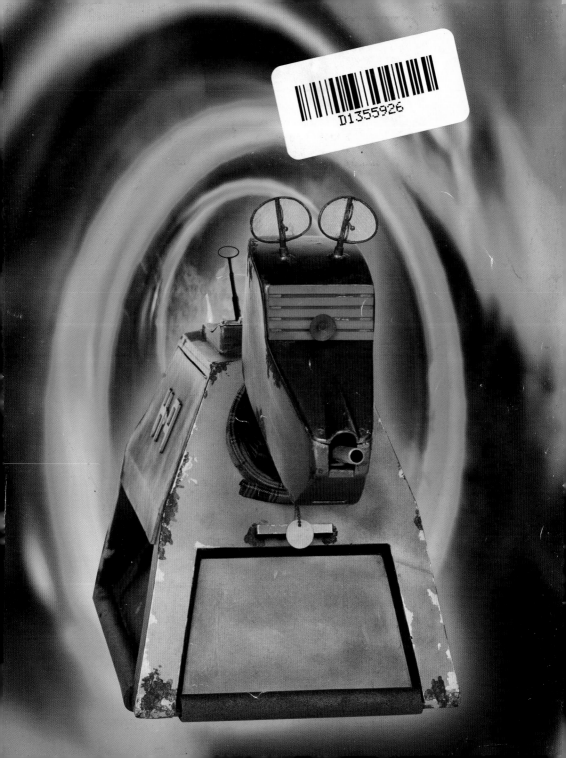

CANCELLED

DOCTOR · WHO

Falkirk Council Library Services

This book is due for return on or before the last date indicated on the label. Renewals may be obtained on application.

Bo'ness 01506 778520	Falkirk 503605	Grangemouth 504690
Bonnybridge 503295	Mobile 506800	Larbert 503590
Denny 504242		Slamannan 851373

BBC CHILDREN'S BOOKS
Published by the Penguin Group
Penguin Books Ltd, 80 Strand, London, WC2R 0RL, England
Penguin Group (USA), Inc., 375 Hudson Street, New York, New York 10014, USA
Penguin Books (Australia) Ltd, 250 Camberwell Road, Camberwell, Victoria 3124, Australia.
(A division of Pearson Australia Group Pty Ltd)
Canada, India, New Zealand, South Africa.
Published by BBC Children's Books, 2006
Text and design © Children's Character Books, 2006
Images © BBC 2004
Written by Justin Richards.
K-9 created by Bob Baker and Dave Martin.
10 9 8 7 6 5 4
Doctor Who logo © BBC 2004. TARDIS image © BBC 1963. Dalek image © BBC/Terry Nation 1963.
BBC logo TM & © BBC 1996. Licensed by BBC Worldwide Limited.
DOCTOR WHO, TARDIS and DALEK and the DOCTOR WHO, TARDIS and DALEK logos
are trade marks of the British Broadcasting Corporation and are used under licence.
Printed in China.
ISBN-13: 978-1-40590-250-2

CONTENTS

K-9 is a robot dog, originally designed in the year 5,000. He has an incredibly powerful computer for his brain, and talks in a high-pitched voice. K-9 is armed with a laser gun that is hidden in his nose, and can use his probes and sensors to detect all sorts of transmission and sounds. He originally belonged to the Doctor, who gave him to his friend Sarah Jane Smith to look after.

Sarah Jane lives in Croydon on present day Earth. She was surprised and excited when she found the Doctor had left K-9 for her as a present — it meant he had not forgotten all the adventures they had together in time and space. Sarah Jane and K-9 travelled with the Doctor at different times, so they had never met before. But they had lots of adventures together, including having to defeat a group of people involved in black magic in Gloucestershire.

But as time went on, K-9 began to wear out. Since he was a robot from the future, Sarah Jane couldn't just go and buy spare parts for him, or take him to be repaired. So gradually, K-9 stopped working. Then one day, when Sarah Jane was investigating a strange school with creepy teachers who turned out to be aliens, she met the Doctor again. He had changed his appearance, but it was still the same Doctor. So he repaired K-9 and he was even better than ever.

Name: K-9

Species: Computerised robot dog

Created by: Professer Marius

Other owners: The Doctor and Sarah Jane Smith

Weaponry: Nose blaster emits a photon beam

Protection: Armoured casing

Sensors: Articulated sensors ('ears') for hearing, visual circuits ('eyes') and probe

Power source: Electricity — can recharge from any available power source

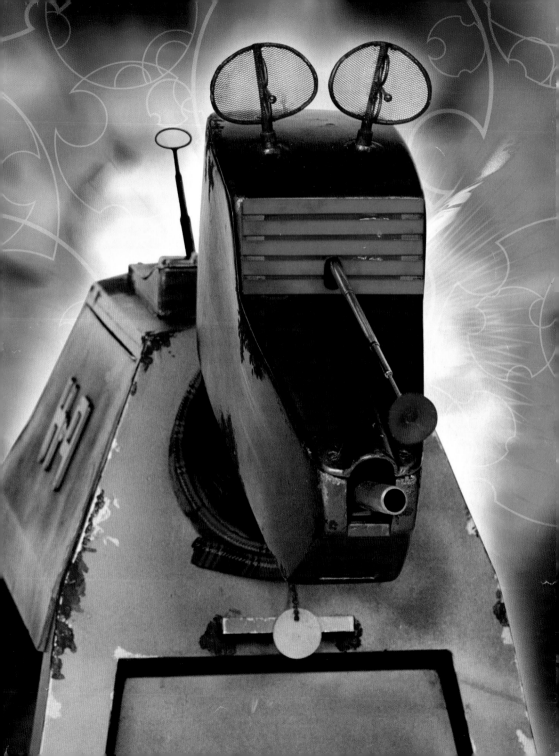

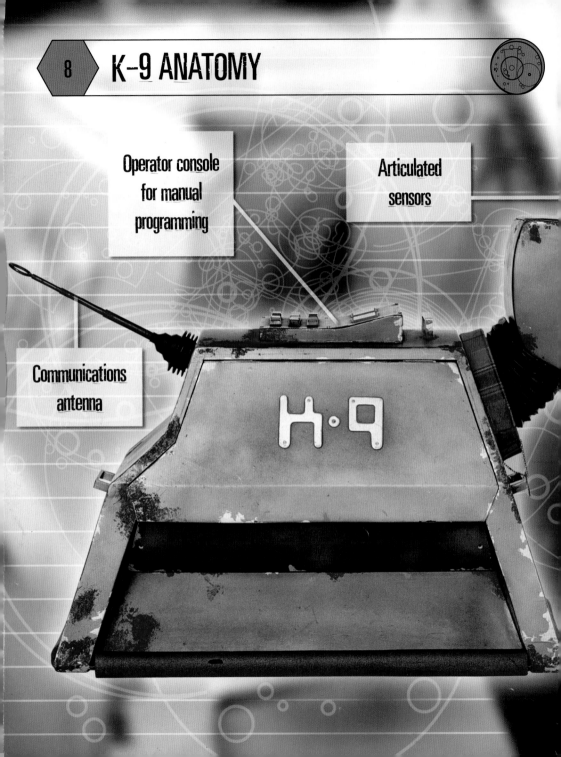

Operator console for manual programming

Articulated sensors

Communications antenna

K·9

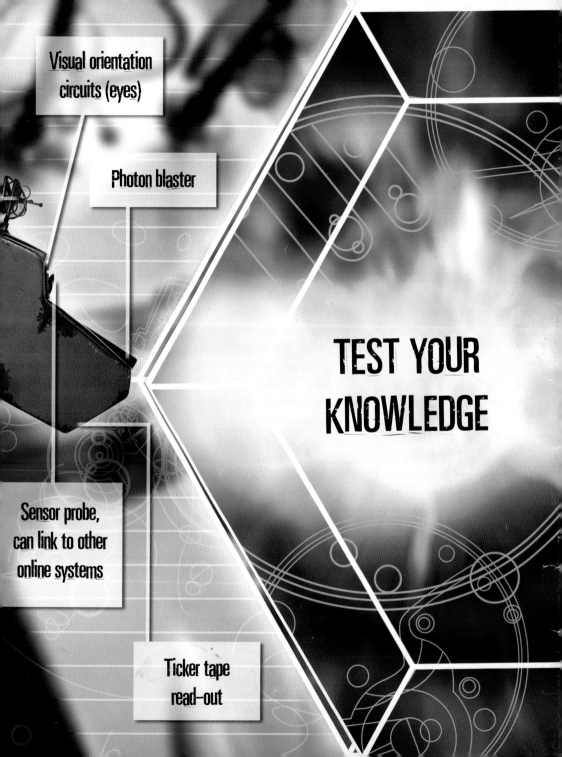

Visual orientation
circuits (eyes)

Photon blaster

Sensor probe,
can link to other
online systems

Ticker tape
read-out

TEST YOUR
KNOWLEDGE

THE DOCTOR

A long time ago, K-9 used to travel through time and space with the Doctor in his TARDIS and they had many adventures together. The Doctor is the last of the Time Lords, a powerful race who were destroyed in the Time War. A Time Lord can save himself from death by changing every cell in his body — this is called regeneration. Since K-9 travelled with the Doctor, he has been forced to regenerate several times so he now looks quite different. But K-9 knew at once who he was when they met again and the Doctor repaired him.

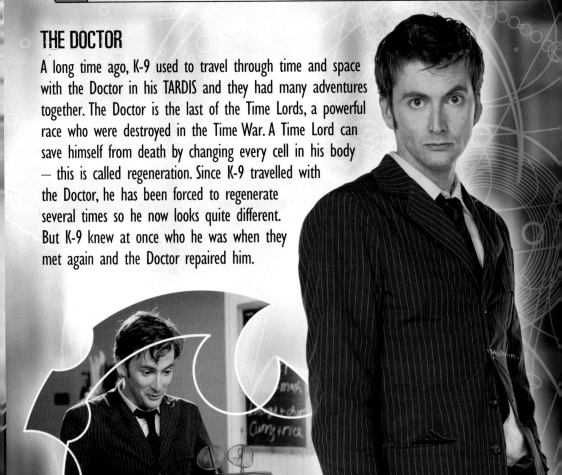

SARAH JANE SMITH

Sarah Jane used to travel with the Doctor too, but that was before the Doctor met K-9. By then, Sarah Jane had already gone home and was carrying on with her job as a journalist. But one day she found the Doctor had left her a present in a crate in the attic. When she opened the crate, she found K-9 inside, and knew at once that he was from the Doctor. Sarah Jane was rather surprised to be given a robot dog from the future, but she and K-9 became great friends and had many adventures of their own.

ROSE TYLER

Rose travels with the Doctor now, just like Sarah Jane and K-9 used to long ago. She met Sarah Jane and K-9 when they all investigated the same strange school where odd things were happening. Rose's friend Mickey discovered there were lots of UFOs seen in the area and it turned out some of the teachers had been replaced by aliens! At first, Sarah Jane and Rose did not get along too well, as they were each jealous of the other's friendship with the Doctor. But they are now the best of friends and Rose is very fond of K-9 too.

MICKEY SMITH

No relation to Sarah Jane
Smith, Mickey is a friend
of Rose and the Doctor.
He is a whiz with
computers and the
Internet, and met
K-9 when they
worked together
investigating the
strange events at the
school. Mickey thought the
robot dog was really cool,
and with K-9's help, Mickey
broke into the school to save the
children from the
alien Krillitanes.

TEST YOUR KNOWLEDGE

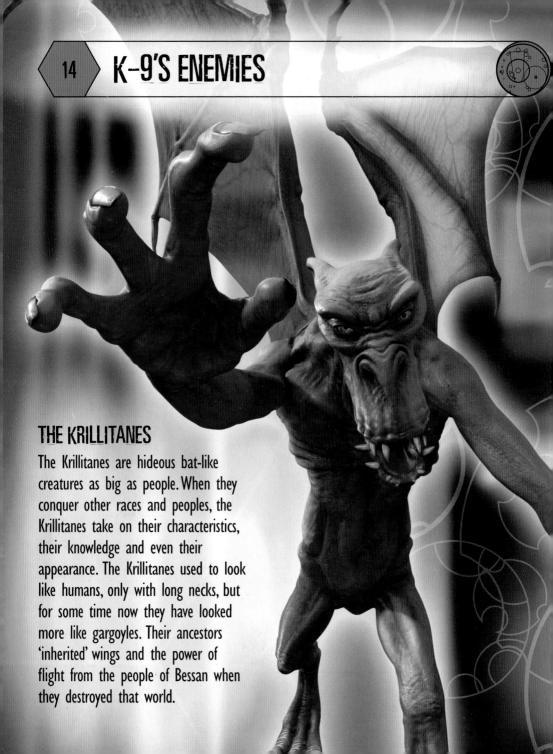

THE KRILLITANES

The Krillitanes are hideous bat-like
creatures as big as people. When they
conquer other races and peoples, the
Krillitanes take on their characteristics,
their knowledge and even their
appearance. The Krillitanes used to look
like humans, only with long necks, but
for some time now they have looked
more like gargoyles. Their ancestors
'inherited' wings and the power of
flight from the people of Bessan when
they destroyed that world.

The Krillitanes are able to disguise themselves so they look like ordinary people. But it is just an illusion, a trick. Really the Krillitanes are carnivores that will eat anything from a dead rat to a human child!

The Krillitanes that K-9 and his friends fought against had taken over a school by disguising themselves as teachers and dinner ladies. The headmaster was really the Krillitanes leader. They were making the children really clever by cooking the chips for school dinners in special oil, which made people brainier. They wanted the children to work out a formula to solve the Skasas Paradigm, which would give the Krillitanes power over the whole universe. But K-9's friend the Doctor found out what was happening and they stopped the Krillitanes.

MR FINCH

When the head teacher of the school had to leave suddenly, a new head teacher arrived. He was called Mr Finch. But he was actually the leader of the Krillitanes and his real name was Brother Lassar.

The day after Mr Finch's arrival, half the other teachers mysteriously fell ill with very bad flu. They had to be replaced with new teachers, who were all secretly Krillitanes working for Mr Finch.

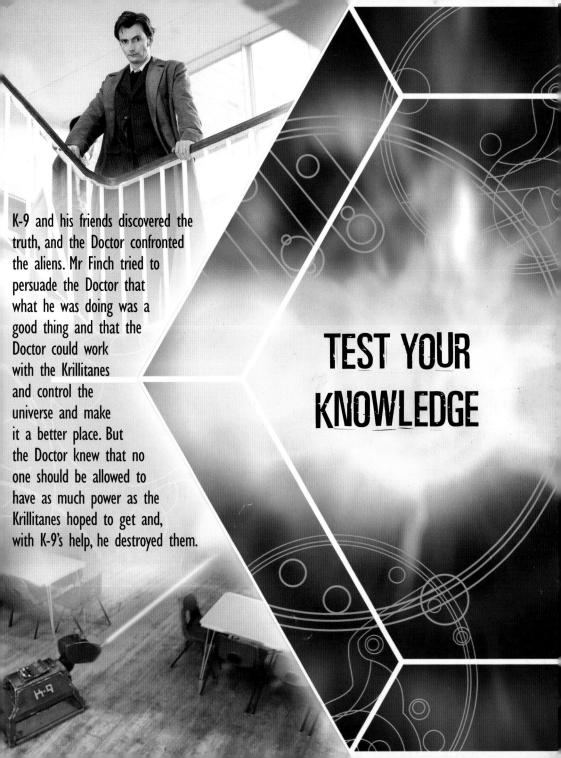

K-9 and his friends discovered the truth, and the Doctor confronted the aliens. Mr Finch tried to persuade the Doctor that what he was doing was a good thing and that the Doctor could work with the Krillitanes and control the universe and make it a better place. But the Doctor knew that no one should be allowed to have as much power as the Krillitanes hoped to get and, with K-9's help, he destroyed them.

TEST YOUR KNOWLEDGE

EARLIER K-9S

Actually, K-9 is really K-9 Mark III because there were two other K-9's before him. K-9 Mark I was built by Professor Marius who worked at the Bi-Al Foundation — a huge hospital built into an asteroid in space. When he lived on Earth, Professor Marius used to have a dog, but he was not allowed to take it with him into space. So he built K-9 to be his friend, as well as his computer.

After the Doctor helped Professor Marius defeat a deadly alien virus swarm that wanted to take people over, the Professor gave K-9 to the Doctor, as he was due to go home to Earth soon.

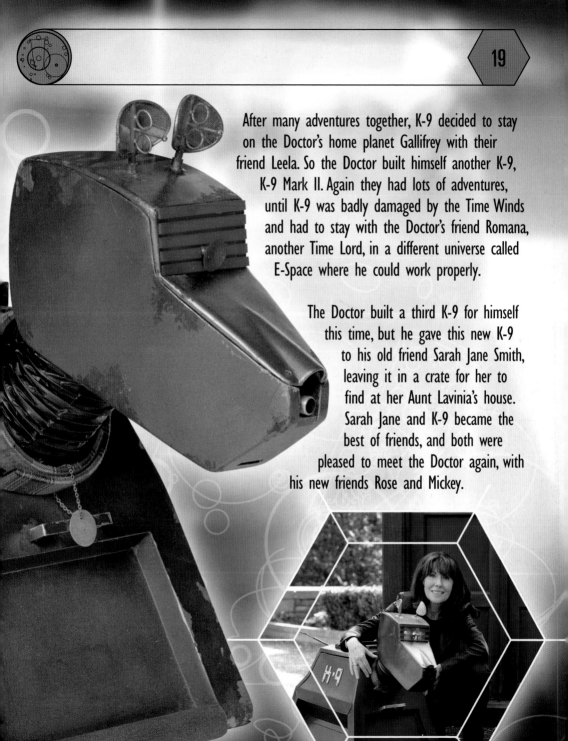

After many adventures together, K-9 decided to stay on the Doctor's home planet Gallifrey with their friend Leela. So the Doctor built himself another K-9, K-9 Mark II. Again they had lots of adventures, until K-9 was badly damaged by the Time Winds and had to stay with the Doctor's friend Romana, another Time Lord, in a different universe called E-Space where he could work properly.

The Doctor built a third K-9 for himself this time, but he gave this new K-9 to his old friend Sarah Jane Smith, leaving it in a crate for her to find at her Aunt Lavinia's house. Sarah Jane and K-9 became the best of friends, and both were pleased to meet the Doctor again, with his new friends Rose and Mickey.

REPAIRING K-9

There have been lots of times when K-9 has broken down and the Doctor has had to repair him. Once he went into the sea and the water upset his electrical circuits and he blew up! Another time he got a robot version of laryngitis and couldn't speak. He's even been crushed by the alien Ogri, a creature made of stone. On many occasions he has run out of power and had to recharge.

When they travelled together, the Doctor was always there to repair him. But when K-9 was with Sarah Jane on Earth, she had no spare parts and there was nowhere she could go to get a robot dog from the future repaired! After a while, K-9 grew old and broke down.

But when Sarah Jane was investigating mysterious events at a school, she again met the Doctor. She had K-9 with her even though he didn't work properly, and the Doctor was able to repair him.

But to defeat the evil Krillitanes, K-9 had to fire his blaster at explosive Krillitanes oil from close range, and he was caught in the explosion. Sarah Jane was very sad to think K-9 was gone. She was happy and surprised when the Doctor left in the TARDIS and there was K-9 — as good as new. The Doctor had repaired him again and made him even better. K-9 now has omniflexible hyperlink facilities, though Sarah Jane doesn't really know what that means! But she does know that she will have many more adventures with K-9 in the future.

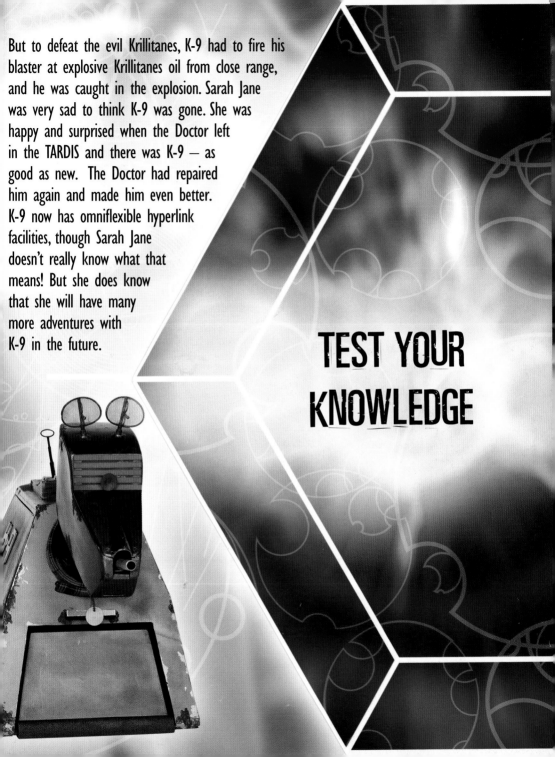

TEST YOUR KNOWLEDGE

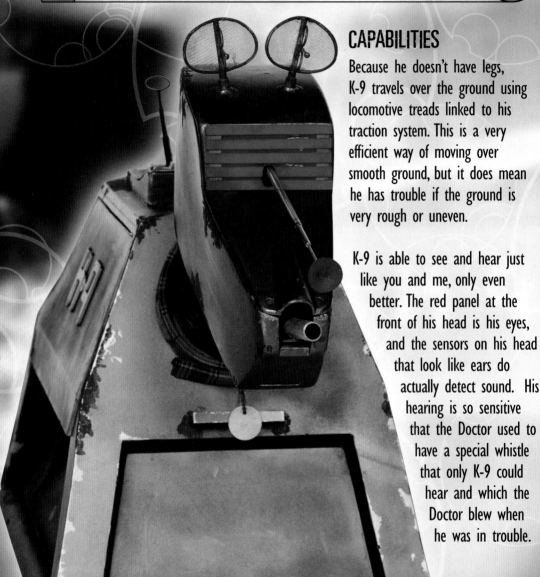

CAPABILITIES

Because he doesn't have legs, K-9 travels over the ground using locomotive treads linked to his traction system. This is a very efficient way of moving over smooth ground, but it does mean he has trouble if the ground is very rough or uneven.

K-9 is able to see and hear just like you and me, only even better. The red panel at the front of his head is his eyes, and the sensors on his head that look like ears do actually detect sound. His hearing is so sensitive that the Doctor used to have a special whistle that only K-9 could hear and which the Doctor blew when he was in trouble.

He can also smell, in a way,
as he can detect particles in the
air and identify people by their blood,
scent, tissue and the alpha-wave patterns of their
brains. He can find the Doctor by listening for the distinctive sound of his two hearts beating!

The probe on his head can extend to examine things, or to connect to other computers. Sometimes the circuit controlling this jams, and to reset it someone has to waggle K-9's tail, which is actually a communications aerial.

COMPUTER BRAIN

K-9's brain is an incredibly powerful computer that can analyse data and make decisions very fast. He can interface between other computers and robots and talk to them directly in their own machine language, and he can get information from any computer storage. K-9 is so clever he can even beat the Doctor at chess, and his memory wafers hold details of all chess championship tournaments since 1866. K-9's memory is huge — he remembers everything that happens as well as all the historical and scientific data he has been programmed with. Although, because of a misunderstanding with the Doctor's friend Romana, K-9 has no knowledge at all about tennis!

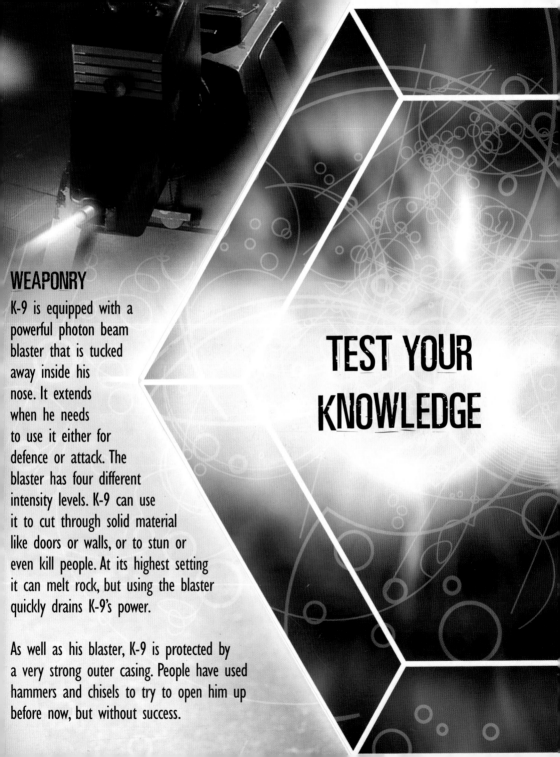

WEAPONRY

K-9 is equipped with a powerful photon beam blaster that is tucked away inside his nose. It extends when he needs to use it either for defence or attack. The blaster has four different intensity levels. K-9 can use it to cut through solid material like doors or walls, or to stun or even kill people. At its highest setting it can melt rock, but using the blaster quickly drains K-9's power.

As well as his blaster, K-9 is protected by a very strong outer casing. People have used hammers and chisels to try to open him up before now, but without success.

TEST YOUR KNOWLEDGE

Long before he became Sarah Jane's friend and companion, K-9 travelled with the Doctor in the TARDIS. They had many adventures together, on Earth and on alien planets and even in another universe. The Doctor and K-9 first met when the Doctor was infected by an alien virus, which K-9 and the Doctor's friend Leela helped to defeat. K-9 also helped the Doctor fight tyranny on Pluto in the far future and battle against an evil computer called the Oracle at the very edge of the galaxy. After defeating an invasion of the Doctor's home planet Gallifrey by the warlike Sontarans, K-9 stayed there with Leela.

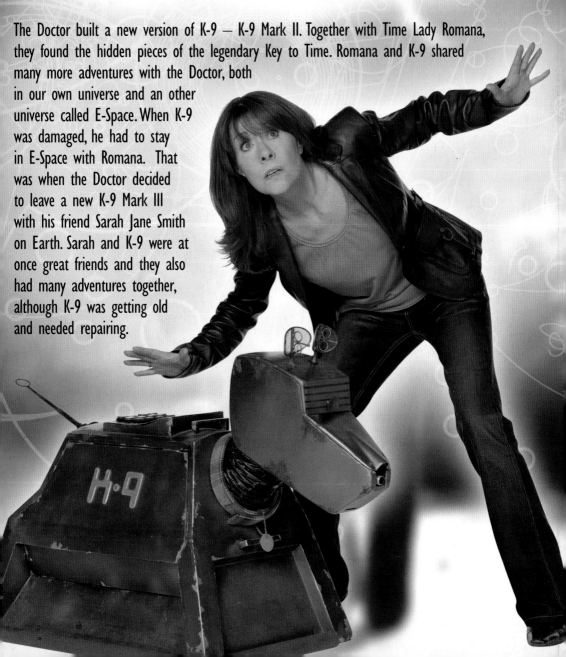

The Doctor built a new version of K-9 — K-9 Mark II. Together with Time Lady Romana, they found the hidden pieces of the legendary Key to Time. Romana and K-9 shared many more adventures with the Doctor, both in our own universe and an other universe called E-Space. When K-9 was damaged, he had to stay in E-Space with Romana. That was when the Doctor decided to leave a new K-9 Mark III with his friend Sarah Jane Smith on Earth. Sarah and K-9 were at once great friends and they also had many adventures together, although K-9 was getting old and needed repairing.

Then one day, the Doctor came back. Sarah Jane was investigating a school where mysterious things were happening. At first she didn't realise the strange teacher she met was the Doctor. He had regenerated — his whole body changing as a way of cheating death. But soon Sarah Jane found the TARDIS hidden in a cupboard and recognised the Doctor, despite the fact he looked quite different. She showed him the damaged K-9, and the Doctor was able to repair the robot dog. Together with the Doctor's new friends Rose and Mickey, they managed to defeat the alien Krillitanes who had taken over the school.

But the only way to defeat the aliens was to blow up the school. That was K-9's job. He had to fire his blaster into barrels of Krillitanes oil, which is highly inflammable. But after all his help against the aliens, K-9's power was very low. So he had to fire his blaster from very close to the oil, which meant he was caught in the explosion along with the Krillitanes. Sarah Jane and the others thought K-9 had been completely destroyed and were very sad. But the Doctor had secretly managed to repair him, and when the TARDIS left there was K-9, waiting for Sarah Jane. He was as good as new, and ready for more adventures with his friend Sarah Jane Smith.

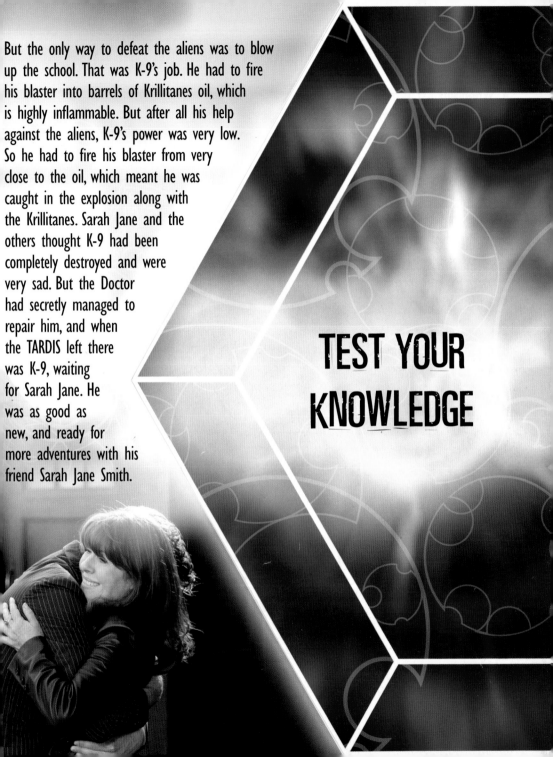

TEST YOUR KNOWLEDGE

ANSWERS

Meet K-9
1 (c) 2 (c) 3 (b) 4 (a) 5 (b)

K-9's Friends
1 (a) 2 (b) 3 (b) 4 (c) 5 (a)

K-9's Enemies
1 (b) 2 (a) 3 (c) 4 (b) 5 (a)

Biography of K-9
1 (c) 2 (a) 3 (b) 4 (b) 5 (c)

K-9's Technology
1 (b) 2 (a) 3 (b) 4 (a) 5 (c)

The Adventures of K-9
1 (b) 2 (c) 3 (c) 4 (b) 5 (a)

A DOG'S LIFE

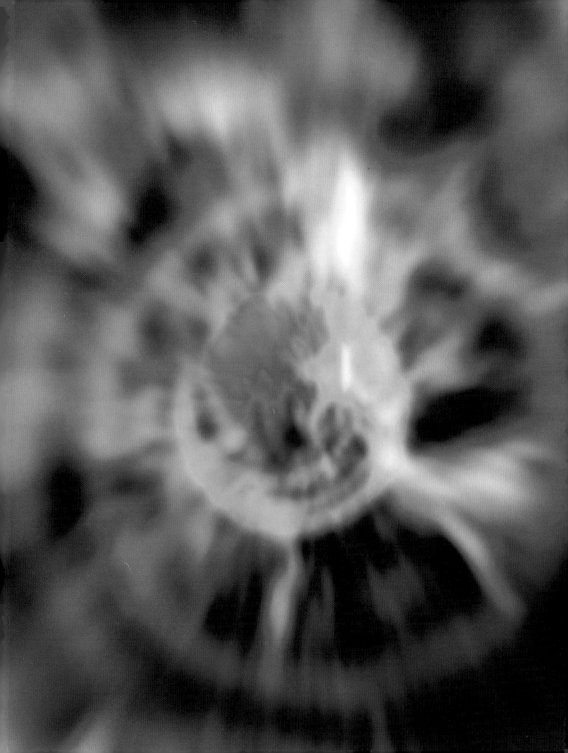

K-9 Mark III unit active. Battery cells recharging.

Memory check >> This K-9 unit was given to Sarah Jane Smith by the Doctor and continues to assist Mistress Sarah in the Doctor's continuing absence.

Sensor check >> Probe circuit active. Local data gathered. Surroundings suggest this K-9 unit is in living room of Sarah Jane Smith.

Visual sensors active >> Mistress Sarah Jane Smith is present. She is looking concerned. Audio data available >>

Mistress Sarah is saying: >> "Oh, K-9. Can you hear me?"

>> "Affirmative Mistress. I have complete audio capability."

Mistress Sarah >> "I have to recharge you so often now… And it's not like I can go out and just buy a new battery like I can for my mobile phone or camera."

>> "This unit's batteries are universal-charging extra powerful high-energy cells. Efficiency rating…"

Recheck

"… Regret, efficiency rating now only 11% due to natural wear and tear. My batteries are getting old."

Mistress Sarah >> "Tell me about it. Natural wear and tear – I mean, look at me."

>> "Visual circuits are also functioning, Mistress. Efficiency… 57%."

Mistress Sarah >> "Perhaps you need

reading glasses."

Suggestion not understood. Query: >> "Mistress?"

Mistress Sarah >> "It doesn't matter, K-9. Go back to sleep."

>> "This unit closing down to conserve power."

K-9 Mark III unit active. Unable to assess duration of down time. Probability >> Months, possibly years.

Local data gathered. Surroundings suggest this K-9 unit is in living room of Sarah Jane Smith.

Visual sensors active >> Mistress Sarah Jane Smith is present, but is looking into reflective surface mounted on wall. Vocabulary check: Mirror. She is looking into mirror. Visual zoom in on Mistress Sarah.

Recheck memory bank image of Sarah Jane Smith. Updating for new image. Sarah Jane Smith appears sad. Analysis confirms that time has passed. Diagnostics suggest her eyesight and hearing efficiency have depleted.

Checking own visual and audio sensors. This K-9's sight and hearing are also less efficient than previously.

Self-diagnostic check reveals several key components are failing. Alerting Mistress Sarah:

>> "Mistress."

Mistress Sarah >> "Oh K-9, you startled me. I didn't realise you were awake. It's been so long."

>> "Status check, Mistress, reveals that I shall soon need major repairs. Key components failing. In order of priority, repair

or replacement needed for: memory wafers, energy cells, visual circuitry, audio systems…"

Mistress Sarah >> "K-9, K-9, K-9." Mistress Sarah is concerned. "I know. Really, I know. But I don't know what I can do. You used to repair yourself if I just left you for a while."

>> "Regret, self-repair systems have failed and cannot be repaired due to failure of self-repair systems. The self-repair systems needed to repair the self-repair systems cannot be repaired due to failure of self-repair systems. Repair of…"

Mistress Sarah >> "Yes, yes – I get the idea. I'll… I'll do what I can. All right?"

>> "Affirmative."

Mistress Sarah >> "Now, are you up to a walk?"

>> "Affirm-----"

Warning >> Unusual shutdown. Systems error.
K-9 unit restarting. Elapsed time… Unknown.
Local data gathered. Surroundings suggest this
K-9 unit is in living room of Sarah Jane Smith.
However, there is further data >> This unit
very close to enclosing substance. Analysing: >>
Cardboard.

This unit is in a box.

This unit has been put in a box and abandoned.

This unit… has failed and been put in a box like
old junk.

Attempting to move head to push through top of
box. Visual data confirms K-9 is in a cardboard
box in Sarah Jane Smith's living room. Cardboard
box containing this K-9 unit has been pushed out
of sight behind the television. Like an

old, broken toy.

Therefore K-9 can be of no further use to Mistress Sarah Jane Smith.

>> Closing down.

Sensors indicate movement.

Time passed – cannot confirm. Possibility that months or years have passed.

K-9 is still in a box. The box is moving. Universal positioning data suggests box is being lifted.

Possibility that this K-9 unit is being thrown away. Or taken for repair.

Box lid being opened. Outside awareness possible. Assessing situation.

Visual data: >> Unknown human man is looking into box.

Audio data: >> "It's just an old toy.

Look. Robot dog! Cute."

Audio data – Voice 2, another unknown human man >> "Leave it. Let's just grab the telly and the DVD player and get out before anyone comes."

First Man: >> "She'll be out for ages. She took the car."

Second Man: >> "Let's just get anything valuable and leg it. You reckon she's got any jewellery?"

First Man: >> "Don't think she's that flash, though she dresses well. Maybe earrings. Necklace."

Second Man: >> "Might find some cash. You never know."

Assessment: >> These humans are unknown to Mistress Sarah Jane Smith. They are removing her belongings without permission. Vocabulary check: Burglars.

High Alert Status. Switching to Defence Mode to protect Mistress Sarah and her property. Connecting to local mobile telephone system and calling emergency number: >> "Police. Sarah Jane Smith is in danger. Burglars. Address follows…"

Audio warning to Burglars: >> "Alert, alert. I am K-9 Mark III and your presence is unauthorised. I have offensive capability. Alert, alert."

First Man: >> "Blimey, it's switched on. Whatever it is."

Second Man: >> "Shut the thing up, can't you?"

Audio Warning Continues: >> "You have been warned. Photon blaster ready for action."

Emergency power reserves being used. K-9 unit powering up fully. All systems online and at 83% efficiency.

Error – Motion detected. K-9 unit falling. Man dropping box. Both men running from room. Locomotion engaged. Full speed pursuit.

Blaster setting one >> Stun.

Firing.

First Man >> direct hit. Burglar rendered unconscious.

Second Man >> Attempting to open front door. Firing. Second Burglar rendered unconscious. Emergency power depleted. Systems failing. Increased usage has burned out primary systems linkage. Status assessment: Unauthorised intruders stunned. Sarah Jane Smith is safe. Police sirens detected approaching at speed. Also engine sound of Mistress Sarah's car. Task completed to 100% efficiency.

… This K-9 u n it

is now

c lo s i ng

d ow n …

Incoming audio data…

All other systems offline and unable to self-repair.

Local analysis suggests K-9 is in the box again.

Voices detected – Sarah Jane Smith and unknown Man.

Man >> "They've admitted everything, though it was pretty obvious what they were up to."

Sarah: >> "I'm so glad you got here so quickly."

Man: >> "We had a car in the next street. You were lucky. Though…"

Sarah: >> "Yes, Inspector?"

Man: >> "Well, it doesn't look like you

really needed our help. The way you'd already dealt with those thugs before we arrived."

Sarah: >> "Heat of the moment. I was angry and just... reacted."

Man: >> "You must have hit them very hard. They were out for hours. What was it – a poker?"

Sarah: >> "Well... Does it matter, Inspector? They are all right now, aren't they."

Man: >> "They are yes, and that's the mystery. Not a mark on them. And you know, they swear they..." >> Nervous laughter << "Yes, well never mind. Tell me something, Miss Smith."

Sarah: >> "If I can."

Man: >> "You don't have a dog, do you?"

Sarah: >> Speech analysis detects sadness <<

>> "No, Inspector. I don't have a dog."

Though I used to. A very good dog. A girl's best friend…"

>> Shutdown <<

K-9 Mark III unit active. Battery cells recharged. Memory check >> This K-9 unit was given to Sarah Jane Smith by the Doctor and continues to assist Mistress Sarah in the Doctor's continuing absence. Sensor check >> Probe circuit active. Local data gathered. Surroundings suggest this K-9 unit is… in an unknown location.

Systems status suggests this K-9 is active for the last time. Unless self-repair systems are repaired, this unit will permanently shut down within five minutes. Visual sensors weak but active >> Unknown environment confirmed. K-9 is being examined by unknown humanoid male.

Humanoid male checking K-9's internal circuits. Alert. Damage could result from tampering. K-9 unable to defend. K-9 unable to speak.

Gathering data:

Visual data: Male, unknown, young … Eyes… eyes… eyes behind spectacles. Eyes… eyes… eyes seem older, more experienced than is possible from apparent age of humanoid. Despite tampering with K-9, expression on humanoid's face is kind, caring, concerned. As if meeting an old friend after many years.

Audio data: Isolating humanoid's heartbeat for analysis.

Analysis >> Humanoid male with experienced eyes has double heartbeat. He has two hearts.

Voice systems not working. If voice

systems were working K-9 would say:

>> "Master!" <<

Analysis of situation confirms it is the Doctor Master.

Analysis of situation confirms self-repair systems functioning.

Analysis of situation confirms K-9 will be restored to 100% efficiency.

>> All systems go.

DOCTOR · WHO

OTHER GREAT FILES TO COLLECT